Original title:
Frost's Embrace

Copyright © 2024 Swan Charm
All rights reserved.

Author: Lan Donne
ISBN HARDBACK: 978-9916-79-504-0
ISBN PAPERBACK: 978-9916-79-505-7
ISBN EBOOK: 978-9916-79-506-4

Wintry Twilight

The dusk drapes softly down,
A blanket of serene gray,
As whispers of the cold wind,
Invite the stars to play.

The trees stand still and bare,
Their branches etched in ice,
While shadows dance like dreams,
A fleeting glimpse of nice.

The ground is crisp and white,
Each step a crunching sound,
A world transformed by magic,
In silence it is found.

The moon a silver coin,
Adorns the night sky clear,
With twinkling lights above,
Its glow is sweet and near.

In wintry twilight's grace,
The heart finds peace within,
As nature holds its breath,
And new beginnings spin.

Veiled in White

The earth wears white's embrace,
A shroud so soft and light,
Each flake a whispered tale,
Of winter's pure delight.

The landscape sparkles bright,
A canvas fresh and wide,
Where every step we take,
Leaves traces of our stride.

The silence is profound,
As snowflakes gently fall,
A tapestry of calm,
That wraps around us all.

The branches bow with grace,
Beneath their frosty coat,
Each tree a sculpted muse,
In winter's soothing note.

Veiled in white we stand,
In wonder of the scene,
Embracing nature's hush,
A moment pure and clean.

Beneath the Frosted Canopy

Underneath the trees' arms,
A world of glistening white,
The frosted canopy glows,
In the soft, tender light.

The air is crisp and clear,
As silence fills the space,
With only whispers heard,
Of winter's warm embrace.

Small critters scurry by,
In search of hidden food,
Their tracks imprint the snow,
In nature's quiet mood.

The branches draped in white,
Are jewels in the sun,
Each sparkle tells the tale,
Of winter's lucid fun.

Beneath this frozen arch,
I wander with a sigh,
In all the magic here,
The heart learns how to fly.

A Symphony of Ice

The world is wrapped in stillness,
A symphony so bright,
Each note a burst of crystal,
That dances in the light.

Icicles like chandeliers,
Adorn the eaves and roofs,
They shimmer with a purpose,
As time unfolds its truths.

The rivers whisper secrets,
As they glide on by,
Their edges framed in beauty,
Beneath the endless sky.

The frozen air is filled,
With music soft and sweet,
A lullaby of winter,
A rhythm none can beat.

In this grand symphony,
The heart aligns with grace,
As nature plays a tune,
In winter's vast embrace.

Sculpted by Winter

In the hush of frosty days,
Branches bow in crystal ways.
Snowflakes dance with gentle grace,
Winter's chill, a cool embrace.

Silent nights with stars aglow,
Shadows glisten, soft and slow.
Footprints vanish in the white,
Nature's art, both pure and bright.

Fires crackle, warm and near,
Stories whispered, sweet and clear.
Cocoa sipped with joyful cheer,
Sculpted dreams as winter nears.

Blankets woven thick and warm,
Hearts entwined from every storm.
Together facing cold's embrace,
Found in winter's softest space.

The Glacial Embrace

Mountains wear a silver crown,
Frozen rivers, beauty found.
Icebergs drift in ocean's sway,
Nature's touch in a ballet.

Crystal castles in the light,
Glaciers gleam, a wondrous sight.
Echoes of a world so still,
Chilled adventures, hearts can fill.

Pine trees draped in snowy white,
Stars above, the world ignites.
Every breath, a frosty mist,
In this realm, none can resist.

Cascading falls, a frozen dance,
Each moment whispers, take a chance.
Glacial tides, they ebb and flow,
In winter's arms, life begins to glow.

Enchanted by the Freeze

A blanket white on every hill,
Crystal dreams, the air is still.
Frozen lakes reflect the skies,
Nature sings in soft replies.

Branches laden with icy jewels,
Winter's breath, a dance of fools.
Every flake a tale untold,
Magic weaves its threads of gold.

Footprints trace a silent path,
Whispers of the aftermath.
Winds entwine, the trees respond,
In the freeze, our hearts are fond.

Frosty patterns on the glass,
Moments frozen, yet they pass.
In this chill, the warmth we find,
Enchanted worlds, forever kind.

Whispers on the Wind

Songs of winter, soft and clear,
Whispers carried far and near.
Frosted pines in twilight's glow,
Gently sway, their secrets flow.

Moonlight dances on the snow,
A tranquil scene, a gentle show.
Each breath visible in the night,
Whispers hold the world so tight.

Breezes hum, a chilling song,
In this realm where dreams belong.
Nature's whispers, sweet and low,
In the winter, life can grow.

Echoes wrap the world in peace,
Wrapped in love that will not cease.
Listening close, the heart expands,
To winter's voice, we take our stands.

Frostbitten Dreams

In the stillness, shadows creep,
Whispers of a winter's keep.
Dreams encased in icy glaze,
Silent sighs through frozen haze.

A world adorned in crystal light,
Timid hearts in frosty flight.
Hopes like snowflakes gently fall,
Fragile wishes, one and all.

Beneath the layers, warmth will dwell,
Hidden tales it longs to tell.
Frosty dreams, they dance and wave,
In the chill, they are so brave.

Crisp white fields, vast and wide,
Nature's chill, a tender guide.
Every breath a fleeting mist,
In this world, we coexist.

As the dawn's first light appears,
Melting away the frozen fears.
In this hour, new dreams take flight,
From frostbitten to warm delight.

Delicate Fragments

Whispers of a springtime breeze,
Cradle moments, gently seize.
Petals falling, colors blend,
Innocence that will not end.

Each fragment holds a vivid tale,
Woven dreams that never pale.
Softly drifting, shades of grace,
In the garden, find your place.

Sunshine kisses every bloom,
Life awakens from its gloom.
Delicate threads in the air,
Fleeting beauty everywhere.

Echoes of a laughter shared,
In this world, the heart is bared.
Moments captured, pure and bright,
Fragments dance in soft twilight.

And in twilight, shadows play,
Delicate as end of day.
Hold the fragments in your hand,
Life's small treasures, oh so grand.

The Quiet Thaw

Winter's grip begins to wane,
Silence breaks with drops of rain.
Gentle whispers, soft and low,
Nature hums a warming flow.

The frozen earth starts to sigh,
Underneath the azure sky.
Green shoots push through icy crust,
In the thaw, we find our trust.

Streams awaken, waters gleam,
Life returns from winter's dream.
Each bud blooms with sweet intent,
Awakening, the heart's lament.

The air is rich with life anew,
Every breath, a vibrant cue.
Colors burst, a joyful sound,
In the thaw, our hopes are found.

And as the quiet days unfold,
Every moment, tales retold.
In the warmth, we find our way,
Through the quiet, into play.

Shards of Serenity

Glimmers found in shards of light,
Reflecting peace, a tranquil sight.
Pieces scattered, yet complete,
In the silence, we retreat.

Gentle ripples on a stream,
A whisper carried like a dream.
Moments held, both near and far,
Each a tiny, guiding star.

Nature's song, a soft embrace,
In the stillness, we find grace.
Shards of joy that dance and play,
Guide us through the light of day.

In the glade where shadows blend,
Amidst the calm, we start to mend.
Every breath, a soothing balm,
In the chaos, find the calm.

And as the evening draws it's veil,
Stillness sings in every trail.
In the quiet, shards align,
Creating peace so divine.

Frost-kissed Reflections

In the morning chill, they gleam,
Mirrored thoughts in winter's stream.
Whispers dance on frozen glass,
Moments trapped as shadows pass.

Silent echoes of the night,
Stars above in shimmering light.
Beneath the frost, a secret sigh,
Nature's breath as crisp winds fly.

Distant mountains etched in white,
Haunting beauty, pure delight.
Each glimmer sings of time's embrace,
A fleeting touch, a soft grace.

Lakes adorned with icy lace,
Holding tales of nature's face.
Frost-kissed dreams in silent peace,
Mem'ries linger, never cease.

Awakening the soul's retreat,
In each corner, calm meets sweet.
With the dawn, new hopes arise,
Beneath the vast and wintry skies.

Petals of Ice

Frozen blooms in crystal hue,
Soft and delicate in morning dew.
Nature's art in winter's chill,
Whispers of time, quiet and still.

Gardens sleep while snowflakes fall,
Silent beauty enchants us all.
Petals scattered in gentle light,
Fragrant dreams take off in flight.

Branches draped in silver sheen,
A wonderland, surreal and serene.
Whirling winds, they tease and play,
Chasing warmth, they drift away.

In the frost, a world so bright,
Glistening under the pale moonlight.
Nature's treasures, oh so rare,
Petals of ice, beyond compare.

Each step stirs the silent ground,
Where winter's secrets can be found.
Beauty blossoms in icy air,
A tranquil pause, a moment rare.

The Sound of Silence

In the stillness of the night,
Whispers echo, lost from sight.
Crystals fall with quiet grace,
Time stands still in frozen space.

Snowflakes dance without a sound,
Blanketing the slumbering ground.
Silent dreams weave through the dark,
As stars ignite with twinkling spark.

Nature holds its breath so deep,
Guarding secrets a world must keep.
In the hush, a heartbeat plays,
Moments linger, soft malaise.

Beneath the frost, life waits concealed,
In silent realms, truths are revealed.
With every sound that fades away,
The heart finds peace in stillness' sway.

A symphony of quiet bliss,
In the twilight's tender kiss.
As night gives way to dawn's bright hue,
Silence speaks in whispers true.

Elegy of Ice

Frozen tears upon the ground,
Echoes of a love once found.
Chilled memories in bitter frost,
Each heartbeat mourns what has been lost.

Ghostly shadows in the mist,
Embraced by winter's frozen kiss.
Loss hangs heavy in the air,
A haunting gaze, a silent stare.

Time remembers all that fades,
In the heart, a cold cascade.
Fingers trace the icy seams,
Fragments linger, lost in dreams.

Amidst the hush, a message clear,
In every sigh, a whispered tear.
Nature mourns with falling snow,
The elegy of what we know.

Yet from the frost, new life will grow,
Through the silence, hope will flow.
In the cycle where endings cease,
Ice will melt, and hearts find peace.

January's Lullaby

Softly falls the winter chill,
A blanket wraps the earth so still.
Whispers of the frosty night,
Embrace the world in silver light.

Stars adorn the midnight sky,
As dreams drift gently, passing by.
A crowd of thoughts begins to fade,
In the hush that winter made.

The moon hums low a tranquil song,
Melodies where hearts belong.
Each flake a note, a soft refrain,
In January's gentle reign.

Fires crackle, embers glow,
Warmth within the icy flow.
Time slows down, the night is long,
In this lullaby, we belong.

So let the frosted beauty stay,
Wrap us tightly, night and day.
In dreams we weave a world so bright,
Within January's soothing light.

Icy Solitude

In the silence, ice does creep,
A world held close, in glacial sleep.
The trees stand bare, in stark array,
Whispers linger, fade away.

Crystal branches shimmer bright,
Glistening beneath the pale moonlight.
Frosty winds begin to sigh,
Carrying tales of days gone by.

Footsteps crunch on frozen ground,
Echoes whisper without sound.
Nature breathes in quiet grace,
Icy solitude, a fleeting embrace.

Clouds meander, shadows play,
In a world where colors sway.
Stillness captured, time stands still,
In solitude, the heart can fill.

Lonely paths beneath the stars,
Inside our hearts, we carry scars.
Yet in the chill, we find our peace,
In icy solitude, our fears release.

Twilight on a Frosty Eve

Twilight dances on the edge,
A moment lingers, pure pledge.
Frosty breath in evening air,
Painting scenes beyond compare.

The sun dips low, a gentle kiss,
In this hour, we find our bliss.
Soft shadows stretch across the land,
Painting pictures, hand in hand.

In the hush, all sounds align,
Nature's canvas, yours and mine.
Stars awaken, twinkling bright,
As we dwell in fading light.

Cold winds weave through night's embrace,
As fireflies dance in a fleeting race.
With every breath, the world transforms,
In twilight calm, our spirit warms.

The night unfolds, a tale untold,
In icy whispers, mysteries old.
We wander forth, hand in hand,
In twilight's hold, we understand.

Whispers Beneath Snow

Beneath the snow, a secret sleeps,
In silent hush, the winter keeps.
Nature's song, a muffled tune,
Whispers soft as the waning moon.

Each flake descends, a gentle grace,
Blanketing the world's embrace.
A tapestry, crisp and white,
Cocooned within the starry night.

Life pauses under frosty veils,
Time stands still in winter's trails.
Echoes fade in icy breath,
Beneath the snow, stories of death.

But in this stillness, life shall thrive,
Hidden dreams, yearning to arrive.
Nature waits for spring's soft hand,
To break the hush across the land.

So let the whispers gently flow,
In the arms of winter's glow.
As the earth rests, hope shall grow,
For life awaits beneath the snow.

Ethereal Blue

In the evening sky, a hue,
Whispers of a dream come true.
Waves of tranquility sweep,
In a world where shadows creep.

Stars like gems in velvet gloam,
Guide the lost ones safely home.
Each twinkle tells a tale anew,
Of love, of hope, in ethereal blue.

Clouds drift softly, thoughts of flight,
Carrying wishes into the night.
Beneath the moon's warm silver lace,
Dreamers find their sacred space.

Tides that kiss the sandy shore,
Echo secrets held before.
In this moment, time stands still,
In the blue, we feel the thrill.

As daylight fades and night unfolds,
Mysteries of life are told.
Wrapped in serenity's embrace,
Ethereal blue—our timeless place.

Charmed by Solitude

In a quiet room, thoughts collide,
Where whispers of solace reside.
Time slows down, the world retreats,
In this haven, my heart beats.

Each thought shapes a story's end,
In silence, I find a friend.
Pages turning with every breath,
In solitude, I conquer death.

Moonlight dances on the floor,
Guiding dreams behind the door.
The pulse of stillness fills the air,
In my heart, I shed despair.

Voices fade, yet echoes stay,
In shadows, hidden truths play.
Charmed by the peace that solitude brings,
I learn to fly on gentle wings.

Graced by moments, oh so rare,
Woven with a tender care.
In the cocoon where fears dissolve,
Charmed by solitude, I evolve.

Ghosts of the Blizzard

Snowflakes weave a tale so grim,
In the chill, memories swim.
Howling winds, a sorrowed sound,
On frozen ground, lost paths abound.

Footsteps echo, shadows dance,
In the storm, there's no second chance.
Whispers linger in the air,
Traces of dreams left somewhere.

Blankets white, a cover deep,
In the night, the lost ones sleep.
Helpless sighs in the swirling frost,
In the blizzard, we count the cost.

Shivered hearts find solace scarce,
Haunted by the winter's glare.
Yet in the gloom, resilience grows,
From the ghosts of the blizzard's throes.

As dawn breaks, the snowflakes fade,
New beginnings unafraid.
In the silence, we find our way,
Leaving behind the ghosts of grey.

Still Waters Run Cold

In the stillness, shadows play,
Ripples form and fade away.
Mirrored skies in quiet grace,
Reflecting time, a gentle pace.

Secrets lie beneath the glass,
Whispers of the moments pass.
Depths conceal what we can't see,
In every wave, a memory.

Calm and cool, the waters flow,
Harboring tales of high and low.
In silence, hearts begin to fold,
As still waters run cold.

Beneath the surface, storms may brew,
Yet here, tranquility rings true.
In liquid depths, the truth unfolds,
In the embrace of waters cold.

With each breath, we calm the tide,
In stillness, we must bide.
For in the heart where silence calls,
Still waters run cold, yet life enthralls.

Memories Entrapped in Ice

In frozen frames of whispered time,
Echoes linger, soft and chime.
Footprints trace the paths we roam,
In winter's grasp, we find our home.

Glimmers stuck in crystalline light,
Reflecting dreams, both day and night.
Heartfelt stories, held in chains,
Bound by frost, where silence reigns.

Ghostly voices in the chill,
Softly calling, memories spill.
Captured joy within the freeze,
Fleeting moments, like the breeze.

Every flake, a tale untold,
Wrapped in white, the past unfolds.
In this silence, we hold tight,
Memories entrapped, pure and bright.

While time whispers, we will keep,
These frozen dreams, both rich and deep.
In stillness, our souls will glide,
Through icebound realms, side by side.

The Last Snowflake's Farewell

A gentle flutter from the skies,
The final flake begins to rise.
It dances down, a soft goodbye,
To winter's hold, with a sigh.

It lands upon a waiting hand,
Melting dreams, like grains of sand.
A fleeting whisper, gone too soon,
Beneath the watchful, silver moon.

In quiet moments, time stands still,
The air is crisp, the world fulfilled.
A soft embrace from winter's breath,
A sigh of life, a kiss of death.

Each snowy petal tells a tale,
Of warmth and love, a gentle veil.
As seasons change, memories stay,
In hearts where the last snowflake lay.

So let it go, this final gift,
As winter fades, our spirits lift.
The last snowflake, a fleeting spark,
In the heart's warmth, it leaves its mark.

Paths of Crystal Light

Through frozen woods, where shadows blend,
Paths of crystal light transcend.
Each step a twinkle, crisp and clear,
Guiding dreams that linger near.

Beneath the boughs of silver white,
We wander softly, hearts alight.
In frosted whispers, secrets flow,
Where nature's peace begins to grow.

The world a canvas, pure and bright,
Imprints of joy, adorned in white.
With every turn, allure unfolds,
In pathways where our story holds.

The air infused with winter's grace,
In every breath, we find our place.
A journey shared, both hand in hand,
Through crystal light, we understand.

So let us roam this quiet scene,
In paths of ice, serene and clean.
Our hearts entwined, we chase the night,
In the beauty of this crystal light.

Echoes of a Winter's Kiss

In twilight hush, the snowflakes fall,
A winter's kiss, a soft enthrall.
Each flake a whisper, pure and light,
In frozen dreams, we find our flight.

With every breath, the world turns white,
An echo in the still of night.
The chill embraces, nature's song,
In winter's arms, we all belong.

Footprints linger on the way,
Hints of joy that lightly play.
In frigid air, this love we chase,
Echoes of warmth, a soft embrace.

Memories dance in frosty air,
In silence shared, we lay bare.
Together woven in this bliss,
We hold the echoes of a kiss.

As dawn approaches, colors bloom,
A gentle thaw dispels the gloom.
Yet in our hearts, the echoes stay,
Of winter's kiss that leads the way.

Ethereal Touch

A whisper through the trees,
Soft as the moonlight's grace,
Dancing shadows intertwine,
In this enchanted space.

Stars flicker, hearts align,
In the silence, secrets dwell,
Each breath, a gentle sigh,
Casts a charming spell.

Misty veils in the dawn,
Carried by the soft breeze,
Awakening the world,
With dreams that aim to please.

Colors in the twilight,
Brush strokes of light and shade,
Whispers of the night air,
In harmony they wade.

Let the spirit wander,
In realms both near and far,
Where time drifts ever lightly,
Beneath a cosmic star.

The Art of Calm

Beneath the quiet sky,
In stillness, we find peace,
Gentle waves caress the shore,
Where worries cease to cease.

Soft whispers of the leaves,
Dance in twilight's embrace,
Time slows its hurried race,
In nature's endless grace.

Moments caught like fireflies,
Flickering in the night,
Each glow a fleeting thought,
A glimpse of pure delight.

Inhaling tranquil air,
We find our hearts aglow,
With every gentle sigh,
The world begins to slow.

Close your eyes, drift away,
To places soft and warm,
Where the art of calm unfolds,
Embracing every charm.

Tales of the Winter Night

Snowflakes kiss the cold ground,
In silence, secrets lie,
Whispers of the winter tales,
Beneath the starlit sky.

Fires crackle, shadows dance,
Stories shared anew,
With every flickering flame,
Magic stirs in the blue.

Blankets wrapped around hearts,
Warming souls inside,
Through windows, frosted dreams,
In chilly winds, they glide.

Moonlight weaves its pattern,
On a landscape dressed in white,
Each shadow tells a story,
Of a long-forgotten night.

Embrace the winter whispers,
Let them fill the air,
For in the tales of silence,
Every moment, we share.

Threads of Chill

Woven in the frosty air,
The chill wraps all around,
With every breath, it dances,
In whispers, it is found.

Crystalline lace on the trees,
Shines under morning light,
Each branch, a story told,
In the heart of winter's night.

Puffs of breath like clouds float,
In laughter, spirits rise,
The world, a canvas painted,
Beneath the smoky skies.

Chilling winds bring tales anew,
Each flake a fleeting dream,
In the echo of our hearts,
Winter weaves her gleam.

So hold close the threads of chill,
Let their magic unfold,
In every frozen moment,
Winter's warmth, pure and bold.

Melodies of the Frigid Air

In the stillness of the night,
Whispers of frost begin to play,
Notes that dance on icy wind,
Echoes of winter's soft ballet.

Stars like diamonds in the sky,
Twinkle through the frosty veil,
Each breath forms a crystal cloud,
Nature's breath, a haunting tale.

Branches bow beneath the weight,
Of snowflakes spun from silver thread,
They sway to the melody,
Of silence where the sun has fled.

An owl hoots in the distance,
A keeper of the frozen night,
While shadows wrap the sleeping earth,
In the glow of pale moonlight.

As dawn breaks with gentle hues,
The air sings of winter's grace,
Melodies fade with the light,
But memories linger in this place.

A Shroud of Silence

In the heart of the broken woods,
Silence drapes like a heavy cloth,
Each whisper lost in the stillness,
A shroud of peaceful, haunting froth.

Shadows stretch on ancient bark,
Time stands still in this sacred space,
Every rustle tells a story,
Of dreams that time cannot erase.

Beneath the canopy of stars,
The night wraps the world in dreams,
Each breath carries the softest prayer,
Where silence reigns and hope redeems.

Footsteps linger on soft moss,
Echoes of a journey far,
With every pause, the heart beats loud,
In the presence of the quiet star.

Yet in the stillness, we must find,
The strength to rise and carry on,
For even in this shroud of peace,
New beginnings greet the dawn.

Fading Footprints

Footprints fade upon the shore,
Waves erase what once was there,
Each step a story left behind,
A memory lost in ocean air.

As tide retreats, the sand reveals,
Ghostly trails of where we've been,
Some etched deep, while others blend,
Into the vastness, blue and green.

Seagulls cry out overhead,
A chorus of the fleeting days,
While sun dips low and shadows stretch,
We chase the light in soft sunrays.

Yet every stride must come to rest,
A journey measured, line by line,
In the sands of time, we find our peace,
As fading footprints intertwine.

So let us wander, hearts unswayed,
For paths may vanish, yet we roam,
Collecting pieces of each day,
In fading footprints, we find home.

Chilling Harmony

Whispers of frost in the air,
Gentle echoes everywhere.
Moonlight glimmers on the ground,
In this peace, we are found.

Branches sway in silent night,
Stars above, so calm, so bright.
A symphony of winter's chill,
Wraps the world in a still.

Snowflakes dance on the breeze,
Nature's hush, a gentle tease.
As we breathe in crystallized air,
This harmony, beyond compare.

Cold winds whisper soft and low,
Carrying tales of the snow.
In the stillness, hearts align,
In this moment, we are fine.

Unity in the quiet night,
The world rests; all feels right.
Every heart, a gentle beat,
In this chilling, sweet retreat.

Underneath the Crystal Layer

Beneath the snow, life takes its rest,
In the silence, nature's best.
Crystal sheets on every tree,
Glisten softly, wild and free.

Frozen dreams beneath the frost,
Wonders hidden, never lost.
Winter's gift, a treasure chest,
Waiting for the spring's bequest.

Hushed whispers of the night,
Blankets warm, soft and white.
Every flake, a story told,
Underneath the blanket cold.

Branches bow with quiet grace,
Nature's breath, a tranquil space.
Echoes linger in the air,
Soft and sweet, everywhere.

In this realm of frozen dreams,
Silence flows like gentle streams.
Underneath the crystal layer,
Life awaits, a silent prayer.

Lingering Frigid Sighs

Frigid breath upon the glass,
Every moment seems to pass.
In the chill, memories pour,
Whispers echoed from before.

Frosted windows paint the view,
Silent stories coming true.
Lingering sighs in twilight glow,
In this time, feelings grow.

Steps imprint in sparkling white,
Each one soft, as if polite.
In the stillness, hearts connect,
Lingering light, we reflect.

Harmonies of winter's call,
In the quiet, we stand tall.
Every breath, a dance in the air,
Lingering moments, beyond compare.

Yet within this frigid sigh,
Warmth ignites, reaching high.
In the cold, we find our way,
Lingering hopes for a bright day.

The Quiet Dance

Snowflakes twirl in silent grace,
Nature's rhythm, slow embrace.
Every step, a soft advance,
In the night, a quiet dance.

Stars above in silver hue,
Watch as dreams are born anew.
In the stillness, we find peace,
This tranquil moment will not cease.

Moonlight bathes the sleeping ground,
In this beauty, we are bound.
Every heart, a beating song,
In this quiet, we belong.

Let the cold wrap us tight,
As we sway in soft moonlight.
Through the night, we move as one,
In this dance, our souls have spun.

Whispers of winter hold us near,
In every step, we conquer fear.
Together in this still expanse,
In the calm, we take our chance.

A Tapestry of White

In the quiet dawn, pure and bright,
Blankets of snow, a wondrous sight.
Crystals dance in the morning light,
Nature's canvas, a sacred rite.

Whispers of peace in the frosty air,
Footprints trail where none would dare.
A world transformed, lovely and rare,
Softly woven, beyond compare.

Branches draped in shimmering grace,
Frozen art in a gentle embrace.
Every corner holds a trace,
Of winter's chill, a cold lace.

Icicles hang from the eaves so tall,
Reflecting sunlight, they glimmer and stall.
Nature's jewels, a silent call,
To pause, to breathe, and to enthrall.

At twilight's end, shadows play,
The sky blushes, hues fade away.
A tapestry brightens the day,
In white perfection, winter's sway.

Glacial Breath

In the depths of frost, time stands still,
Whispers of ice on the frozen hill.
Beneath the surface, the world can thrill,
With glacial breath, nature's chill.

Avalanches hush in the silent night,
Stars twinkle down, burning bright.
Moonlight dances, a silver light,
As shadows melt from the icy bite.

Crystal rivers carve the stone,
In ancient tales, they are known.
Glacial streams, a gentle tone,
Flowing smoothly, never alone.

The air, so crisp, a biting sting,
Where frost is born, and cold winds sing.
Nature's symphony, in a ring,
Of icy notes, a wondrous thing.

As morning breaks with golden hues,
The world awakens, fresh and new.
In glacial breath, we find our views,
Of beauty deep, in frosty cues.

Serene Subzero

Underneath the frozen skies,
Whispers murmur, softly rise.
In serene subzero's sighs,
Nature's secrets harmonize.

Fields of white, a tranquil sea,
Where silence breathes naturally.
A world untouched, wild and free,
In winter's grasp, eternity.

Crystalline patterns grace the trees,
Dancing softly in the breeze.
Every flake, a masterpiece,
Colder moments seek to please.

Starry nights bring peace profound,
In the stillness, magic found.
Chasing echoes, all around,
In subzero's embrace, we're bound.

Yet as the dawn greets us anew,
Beneath the frost, life starts to brew.
Serene subzero will renew,
As warmth returns, with skies of blue.

Twilight on Ice

As daylight fades, soft shadows blend,
The ice reflects where colors send.
In twilight's hush, the night descends,
Crafting wonders that never end.

Ghostly figures dance and twirl,
Moonlit waves in a fluid swirl.
Silver linings, the frost pearls,
In the stillness, magic unfurls.

Gliding whispers on crystal floors,
Over landscapes, where silence soars.
Stories dormant, behind closed doors,
Awaken gently, as spirit roars.

A frigid breath in the mellow night,
Hand in hand with the fading light.
Nature's canvas, a beautiful sight,
Painting dreams as stars ignite.

From dusk to dawn, the beauty stays,
In twilight's charm, we find our ways.
On ice we tread, through the haze,
A fleeting moment, forever plays.

Dance of the Winter Night

Beneath the silver moon's soft light,
Snowflakes twirl in joyful flight.
Whispers sway in the chilly breeze,
Nature's rhythm, calm and free.

Frozen branches gently sway,
As winter's magic holds the day.
The stars above begin to gleam,
In this serene and peaceful dream.

Footprints mark the snowy ground,
Where laughter lingers all around.
Children play, their spirits bright,
In the dance of the winter night.

Fires crackle while tales unfold,
Warm hearts bask in winter's hold.
With every sip of cocoa sweet,
We find our joy in the cold's retreat.

As twilight fades, the world awaits,
The beauty of winter celebrates.
In this dance, we find our place,
Amidst the cold, a warm embrace.

Silent Icicles

Hanging like jewels from the eaves,
Silent icicles, winter weaves.
Glistening in the morning light,
A frozen art, pure and bright.

They drip in time with a quiet song,
Nature's symphony, serene and strong.
Each drop a note, a tender chime,
In harmony with the rhythm of time.

Silent soldiers in the winter's grasp,
Holding secrets in their chilly clasp.
They shimmer softly, a tranquil sight,
Guardians of the long winter night.

Through the stillness, whispers flow,
Tales of warmth where memories grow.
In the thaw, they softly fade,
Leaving only the warmth they made.

In the quiet, they stand tall,
A testament to winter's call.
Icicles shining, stories to share,
In the heart of the cold, love is rare.

The Cold Embrace of Solitude

In the stillness of the night,
Solitude wraps me, pure and tight.
The world outside is hushed and deep,
In this silence, secrets keep.

Snow blankets all, a gentle shroud,
Wrapping dreams beneath a cloud.
The whispering winds, soft and low,
Carry echoes of long-lost glow.

A single candle's flame does flick,
Casting shadows that dance and trick.
With each breath, the world feels wide,
In solitude, I calmly bide.

Gone are the crowds, the bustling sound,
Here in the cold, peace is profound.
The heart reflects on what once was,
In solitude, I find my cause.

Through the frost, my spirit roams,
In every flake, I find my homes.
The cold embrace is where I grow,
In winter's heart, my soul does flow.

Under the Snow-Laden Sky

Under skies so gray and wide,
Snowflakes drift with quiet pride.
Each one tells a tale of old,
Of winter's magic, brave and bold.

Trees wear coats of sparkling white,
A wondrous, glittering delight.
The world transformed, so still, so pure,
In this beauty, we feel secure.

Children laugh with joy untold,
As they watch the snow unfold.
A world awash in hues so bright,
Underneath the soft, snow-laden night.

Each breath is a cloud, crisp and clear,
As winter whispers in our ear.
The night unfolds, calm and shy,
Under the vast, snow-laden sky.

In this moment, time stands still,
As hearts are filled with winter's thrill.
With stars that twinkle from afar,
We gather close, under night's star.

Winter's Whisper

Softly falling snowflakes,
Dance upon the silent ground.
Whispers of the winter's breath,
Hushed in twilight, dreams abound.

Barren branches arch and bow,
Clad in coats of silver sheen.
The world wears a quiet shroud,
Wrapped in white, serene and keen.

Frosty winds begin to sigh,
Carrying the secrets old.
In the chill, the spirits fly,
Tales of warmth and love retold.

Night descends with crystal stars,
Glistening on the frozen lake.
Echoes of the past are ours,
In the stillness, hearts awake.

As the dawn breaks, shadows fade,
A gentle light begins to rise.
Winter's grip will soon cascade,
Into spring's embrace, we prize.

Chilled Reverie

In the stillness of the night,
Cold breaths weave through dreams so clear.
Frosty air invites delight,
Embracing what we hold dear.

Candles flicker, shadows dance,
Casting warmth upon the walls.
In this moment, lost in trance,
Winter's call, a gentle thrall.

Blankets piled, we burrow deep,
Hot cocoa warms our frozen hands.
Through the window, starlights peep,
Painting tales across the lands.

Snowflakes tremble as they fall,
Whispers of a soft embrace.
Nature's hush, a soothing call,
Capturing time's tranquil grace.

Together in this frosty world,
Hearts entwined, we find a way.
In the beauty, love's unfurled,
Chilled reveries here to stay.

Embrace of Ice

Crystals glimmer in the sun,
Nature wrapped in chilled delight.
A landscape where the rivers run,
Frozen dreams in winter's night.

Breathe in deep the frosty air,
Feel the bite upon your skin.
Every breath a whispered prayer,
In the silence, magic's kin.

Tree limbs laden, burdened soft,
Snowy blankets draped with care.
In this realm, the spirits loft,
Dancing lightly in the air.

Night descends, the world in peace,
Stars adorned with frosty lace.
In this hush, our worries cease,
Embrace of ice, a slow grace.

As the twilight fades to gray,
Hopes arise with dawning light.
Winter nights must fade away,
Giving way to spring's delight.

The Quiet Thaw

Gentle warmth begins to rise,
Underneath the melting snow.
Birdsong weaves through morning skies,
Nature whispers, soft and slow.

Streams awaken from their sleep,
Trickling down the valley's spine.
New life stirs from winter's keep,
As the sun begins to shine.

Blossoms peek through icy seams,
Color breaks the monochrome.
Hope and beauty feed our dreams,
Rooted deep, they find a home.

In the air, a fragrant breath,
Promises of life anew.
From the frost, we rise from death,
Bidding winter's chill adieu.

Underneath the azure dome,
Joy returns, the earth's rebirth.
In the heart, we find our home,
Through the thaw, we find our worth.

Crystals in the Moonlight

In the night, the crystals gleam,
Casting smiles, a silvery dream.
Stars above in silent sweep,
Whisper secrets, soft and deep.

Gentle winds, they swirl and play,
Dancing lights to guide our way.
Moonbeams stretch on fields of white,
Embracing all in tender light.

Reflections drip from trees so bare,
Each one holds a tale to share.
Glistening softly, nature's art,
With every shimmer, stirs the heart.

Amidst the quiet, shadows sway,
Branches bend, as if to say,
Winter's breath, so crisp and clear,
Weave a magic, drawing near.

In this realm of night so grand,
Crystals speak, though not a hand.
Finding peace in moonlit grace,
Embracing joy in this lost place.

The Soul of Winter's Breeze

Whispers weaving through the trees,
The soul dances with each breeze.
Softly sighing, tenderly near,
Carrying secrets, sharp and clear.

Footprints traced in glistening snow,
Memories linger, fast and slow.
A chilling kiss upon the cheek,
Echoes of the stillness, meek.

With every gust, a story told,
Of nights wrapped in blankets, bold.
Fires crackle, warmth inside,
While shadows of the night coincide.

Snowflakes twirl in playful spin,
A haunting serenade begins.
Each frozen breath, a work of art,
The winter's soul, within the heart.

Upon the peaks, the silence reigns,
Carving beauty in winter's chains.
Embrace the chill, the fleeting peace,
In winter's song, we find release.

Where Cold Shadows Meet

In the twilight where shadows blend,
Whispers linger, gently bend.
A world where warmth begins to fade,
Wrapped in silence, dreams are laid.

Paths of frost weave through the night,
Echoing stars, a distant light.
Footsteps hush on icy ground,
In this realm, lost souls are found.

Branches clasp with tender grace,
Nature's bones in a frozen embrace.
Where the cold and dark align,
Brooding spirits intertwine.

Reflections dance in night's cold grip,
Glimmers on this frosty trip.
Each shadow holds a story's beat,
In the stillness where cold shadows meet.

Here, the heart learns to unwind,
Finding warmth in the night so blind.
As dawn beckons with soft retreat,
The world awakens, bittersweet.

Frostbitten Dreams

In the depth of winter's night,
Frostbitten dreams take gentle flight.
Chilled whispers brush against the skin,
Inviting tales of where we've been.

Each breath, a crystal drawn with care,
Moments frozen in silent air.
Nostalgia blooms in drifts of white,
Softly glowing under moon's bright light.

Sleepy echoes, shadows roam,
Wandering far from their warm home.
In every flake, a story packed,
A world of dreams, silently stacked.

Underneath the blanket's sway,
Frostbitten thoughts refuse to play.
While outside, winter's grip holds tight,
Inside, we forge our own delight.

So let the chill cradle the hours,
As dreams unfold like winter flowers.
In this season's serene embrace,
Frostbitten dreams find their place.

Echoes of the Frozen

In winter's grasp, the silence grows,
Whispers dance where the cold wind blows.
Shadows sidle through the ice,
Memory's touch feels cold as spice.

A world encased in ethereal light,
Footprints vanish into the night.
Echoes linger in frosted air,
Beauty found in the starkest care.

Brittle branches, a crystal waltz,
Nature pauses, but never halts.
Each breath a ghost in the frozen space,
Time slips gently, leaving no trace.

Snowflakes weave a delicate song,
Every flake, where dreams belong.
Frozen moments, a fleeting chance,
In their stillness, the heart can dance.

So here within this icy dome,
Every echo feels like home.
The frozen world holds secrets tight,
In solitude, we find our light.

Stillness in White

A blanket drapes the earth so wide,
Embracing silence, stillness inside.
Fields of white, a tranquil sight,
Soft and gentle, day turns to night.

Winter whispers secrets slow,
Through the trees, where cold winds blow.
In the hush, a heartbeat sounds,
Life still stirs beneath the grounds.

Frozen rivers, a mirror's grace,
Reflecting stars in a darkened space.
Footfalls muffled, peace prevails,
In this quiet, the heart exhales.

Shadows stretch on the pale expanse,
Time stands still in a frosty trance.
Every breath a crystalline hue,
Wrapped in silence, me and you.

So let us cherish moments pure,
In white stillness, we can endure.
Together, finding warmth in cold,
Stories whispered, gently told.

The Dancer's Solitude

In moonlit night, she twirls alone,
Softest whispers, a breath, a moan.
Each graceful move, a fleeting trace,
In solitude, she finds her place.

Twirling shadows, a spectral glow,
Fingers touch the dream's warm flow.
With each spin, the world dissolves,
A dancer's heart, through silence, evolves.

Music echoes in the midnight air,
Notes entwined with the winds of care.
Footsteps light, like falling snow,
In the stillness, her spirit glows.

A moment caught, forever held,
In whispered dreams, her heart is swelled.
Alone yet free, in dance she thrives,
In solitude, her beauty dives.

The stage is bare, but she ignites,
With inner fire, through the nights.
In her dance, she finds the whole,
The quiet music of her soul.

Frosted Labyrinths

Amidst the trees, a pathway winds,
Covered in white, where mystery blinds.
Footprints lead to nowhere near,
In frost's embrace, the heart feels sheer.

Each turn conceals a tale untold,
Whispers of ghosts woven in cold.
Branches guard their secrets tight,
As shadows dance in the fading light.

Labyrinths spun from icy breath,
A path that dances with hints of death.
Yet in the chill, beauty abounds,
Ethereal light in the snow surrounds.

With every step, a challenge posed,
Frosted whispers, the path enclose.
Finding solace in nature's maze,
In frozen moments, we seek to gaze.

Through winding trails, the heart does roam,
In frosted beauty, we find our home.
Each labyrinth holds a truth to claim,
In winter's arms, we stoke the flame.

Snowbound Whispers

Softly falling, whispers glide,
Through the branches, snowflakes bide.
In the hush, a secret sigh,
Winter's breath, a lullaby.

Footprints mark the silent ground,
In the silence, peace is found.
Frosty edges, sparkling bright,
Nature's canvas, pure delight.

Branches bow with silver weight,
Glistening dreams, a quiet fate.
Every flake, a story spun,
Underneath the pale, cold sun.

Whispers floating, soft and slow,
In the twilight's gentle glow.
Frozen echoes, thoughts entwined,
In the stillness, hearts aligned.

Snowbound realms, a world anew,
Wrapped in white, a tranquil view.
In the night, the stars are bright,
Guiding souls with soft moonlight.

Glimmer in the Gloom

In the shadows, a spark appears,
Whispers of hope, quiet cheers.
Through the dark, a glimmer grows,
Warming hearts as the night flows.

Silver threads in the twilight weave,
Softly urging us to believe.
Every glint, a promise cast,
A light to guide us through the vast.

Fleeting moments, shadows dance,
Inviting us to take a chance.
With each flicker, fears dissolve,
In the mystery, we evolve.

Golden whispers through the trees,
Carried gently by the breeze.
In the gloom, we find our way,
Led by light that will not sway.

With each step, the darkness fades,
In the glow, new hope cascades.
Together, strong, we find our tune,
Dancing beneath the watchful moon.

Treetops Adorned

Treetops dressed in emerald hue,
Kissed by sunlight, fresh with dew.
Leaves fluttering in gentle breeze,
Nature's canvas, hearts at ease.

Birds take flight, a joyful song,
In the boughs where they belong.
Branches sway, a graceful dance,
Inviting all to take their chance.

Shadows play upon the ground,
In this realm, peace can be found.
Amidst the trunks, whispers roam,
Calling us to find our home.

Glimmering thoughts in dappled light,
Every moment feels so right.
Hands reaching for the sky above,
Beneath the leaves, a world of love.

As the day drifts into night,
Treetops glow with stars so bright.
In the stillness, dreams take flight,
Adorned in magic, pure delight.

The Enchanted Chill

Whispers of winter roam the air,
In the stillness, secrets share.
Frigid breaths on rosy cheeks,
Nature's hush, the heart it seeks.

Frosty patterns on windowpanes,
Drawing stories in cold remains.
Every breath, a cloud of white,
Embraced by the enchanted night.

Under stars, the world serene,
Wrapped in shadows, softly seen.
Crystalline dreams, a frosty thrill,
In the silence, time stands still.

Glistening trails of icy streams,
Whispers echo with soft screams.
In the chill, the magic glows,
Every heartbeat, winter knows.

As the moon casts silvery beams,
Hope awakens from our dreams.
In the cold, warmth starts to spill,
Through the heart of the enchanted chill.

A Tapestry of White

Snowflakes dance like whispered dreams,
Covering branches in silent gleams.
A quilt of white on the earth's embrace,
Nature's canvas, a tranquil space.

Each breath a mist in the frosty air,
Footprints echo in the cold, so rare.
Beneath the sky of a silver hue,
Every moment feels fresh and new.

Twilight falls with a gentle sigh,
Stars peek out from the velvety sky.
The world transformed, serene and bright,
In winter's arms, the heart takes flight.

Crisp and clear, the evening calls,
As shadows stretch, the daylight falls.
In this hush, the magic stirs,
Wrapped in peace, the spirit purrs.

A tapestry woven with threads of frost,
In every corner lies beauty embossed.
A fleeting glimpse of the season's grace,
In winter's hold, we find our place.

The Shimmering Chill

Frosty whispers through the trees,
A sparkling blanket in the breeze.
Cold air nips at cheeks aglow,
As twilight paints the world below.

The moonlight dances on the snow,
Shimmering patches, a gentle flow.
Each glimmer tells a tale of night,
In the stillness, a quiet light.

Brittle branches, wrapped in white,
Glimmer softly in the fading light.
Under starlit skies, dreams take shape,
In the chill, the heart escapes.

A world of wonder, frozen tight,
Where every shadow gleams so bright.
Nature sleeps in a crystal bed,
With sparkling visions in its head.

Each step a crunch, a symphony,
In this realm of tranquility.
The shimmering chill, like a soft embrace,
Holds us close in winter's grace.

Glacial Serenity

Icicles hang with a graceful sway,
Reflecting light in a clear display.
Mountains stand like ancient guards,
Wrapped in blankets of frosty shards.

Silent valleys, so vast and deep,
In winter's hold, even shadows sleep.
The air is crisp, pure as the chance,
To witness nature's quiet dance.

Glistening rivers, frozen still,
Capture moments against their will.
Whispers echo through the air,
In glacial serenity, we share.

A canvas white, untouched, untouched,
In every corner, beauty clutched.
The heart finds peace where beauty lies,
Underneath the vast winter skies.

Echoes of silence, soft and sweet,
Each heartbeat syncs with the world's beat.
In glacial realms, we pause and breathe,
Finding solace in what we weave.

Winter's Grasp

In winter's grasp, the world stands still,
As shadows lengthen on the hill.
The chill of night wraps close the day,
In frosted breaths, the warmth drifts away.

Starlit skies in crisp repose,
Whispers of snow where the soft wind blows.
Beneath the blanket, life's pulse slows,
In cozy corners, our peace grows.

Each flake dances, a fleeting guest,
Laying still as the world takes rest.
With every breath, the magic flows,
As winter's grasp gently bestows.

Trees wear coats of shimmering white,
A breathtaking scene beneath the night.
The heart ignites with a winter's fire,
As we embrace the cold desire.

Through frosty pastures, we roam and play,
Finding joy in the light of day.
In winter's grasp, we hold on tight,
To the beauty of the starry night.

Dancing in a Winter Wonderland

Snowflakes swirl in frosty air,
Laughter rings, a joyful share.
Children play with hearts so light,
Dancing through the sparkling night.

Trees adorned in purest white,
Moonlight casts a silver light.
Footprints mark the path we tread,
In this dream where joy is spread.

Warming fires greet the cold,
Embers whisper stories told.
Hot cocoa warms our chilly hands,
As we roam these winter lands.

Sprightly spirits all around,
In this magic, love is found.
Together, we embrace the chill,
In our hearts, the warmth will fill.

Snowflakes gather, soft and deep,
Moments cherished, ours to keep.
Dancing on this frozen ground,
In this wonderland, we're bound.

Shimmering Snowflakes

Falling softly from the skies,
Whispers float like lullabies.
Each unique, a fleeting grace,
Nature's art in pure embrace.

Glimmers shine in morning light,
Painting landscapes, pure and bright.
Colors dance in frosty air,
A delicate and wondrous flare.

On the ground, they gently lie,
A soft blanket where dreams fly.
Underneath the vast gray skies,
Shimmering, a secret prize.

Catch them lightly on your tongue,
Feel the joy when you are young.
Snowflakes twirl in playful flight,
Kissing cheeks with pure delight.

When the evening shadows creep,
Snowflakes drift and softly sleep.
In their stillness, magic grows,
Whispers of the world it knows.

The Icy Heart

In the depths of winter's grace,
Lies a heart that hides its face.
Frozen tears of sorrow's plight,
Veiled beneath the soft moonlight.

Chilled to bone, the silence speaks,
Within the soul, a shadow peeks.
Longing warmth in every beat,
Yet fear keeps it incomplete.

Walls of ice, a fortress tall,
Guarding dreams from winter's call.
But in the cold, a spark remains,
A fragile light through icy chains.

Hope will thaw these frozen streams,
Melt away the hardest seams.
With every breath, it yearns to start,
A journey from this icy heart.

Softly, spring will weave its thread,
Breaking chains where ice has bled.
And love will come, a warming art,
Embracing all this icy heart.

Glistening Echoes

In the quiet of the night,
Whispers glisten, pure delight.
Echoes of a laughter past,
Trace the paths, so deep, so vast.

Twinkling stars above us shine,
Guiding dreams that intertwine.
Each soft breath, a memory,
Glistening like the endless sea.

Silent woods, a canvas bright,
Echoes dance in flickering light.
Every moment calls us near,
In this space of warmth and cheer.

Glistening steps on frosty ground,
Nature's symphony profound.
With each heartbeat, stories flow,
In the echoes, love will grow.

Hold these glimmers, hold them tight,
In the shadows, find the light.
Through the silence, we will weave,
Glistening echoes will believe.

Crystals in the Moonlight

In the night, the crystals gleam,
Reflecting softly in a dream.
Whispers dance on silver rays,
Guiding hearts through shadowed ways.

Moonlight spills like liquid grace,
Cascading down to warm embrace.
Each facet tells a story clear,
Of hidden hopes and cherished fear.

A gentle glow on icy ground,
Every breath a hush profound.
Nights alive with sparkling sights,
Lost in the magic of the nights.

Stars above the tranquil sky,
Lull the world, let silence lie.
Crystals twinkle, dreams take flight,
In the serenity of night.

With every glimmer, souls awake,
In the moonlit tapestry we make.
Crystals shining, spirits rise,
Beneath the vast and starry skies.

The World's Slumber

When darkness falls, the world retreats,
In soft embrace, the heart still beats.
Silent dreams on pillows rest,
In tranquil cocoon, the mind is blessed.

Candlelight flickers, shadows play,
Melodies of night begin to sway.
Crickets sing their lullabies,
Underneath the starry skies.

The moon looks down with tender eyes,
While gentle winds breathe soft goodbyes.
Nature whispers, hush, be still,
As night unfolds its quiet thrill.

The world's wrapped in a velvety shroud,
Veils of peace that calm the crowd.
In every corner, dreams may bloom,
In this silent, sacred room.

Rest now, dear, let worries cease,
In slumber's grasp, discover peace.
With dawn's light, new hopes will stir,
But for now, let night confer.

Beneath the Hush

Underneath the evening sky,
Softly where the whispers lie.
Nature holds her breath so tight,
Embracing all within her light.

Stars appear like scattered seeds,
Filling hearts with gentle needs.
In the stillness, dreams take flight,
Beneath the hush of pure delight.

Moments pause, the world stands still,
Savoring night's enchanting thrill.
Moonbeams dance on dewdrop lace,
Painting shadows in soft grace.

Every rustle, breath, and sigh,
Tells a tale as time drifts by.
In this calm, the soul feels free,
Beneath the hush, we simply be.

Listen close, the night will speak,
To the heart that learns to seek.
In silence, find the magic pure,
Beneath the hush, we can endure.

Caught in the Chill

Winter wraps its fingers tight,
Biting winds in the pale moonlight.
Breath like smoke in the frosty air,
Whispers echo, yet none are there.

Trees stand bare, their arms held high,
As flakes of snow gently sigh.
Caught in chill, the world slowed down,
A sleepy hush envelopes town.

Silent footsteps on the ground,
Frozen dreams in silence found.
Each moment drifts like falling snow,
In tranquil peace, the heart will grow.

With every flake, pure magic spills,
Quiet contentment in winter's thrills.
Caught in time, the beauty steals,
In the calm, a warmth reveals.

Stars shimmer like diamonds bright,
In the depths of the tranquil night.
Caught in the chill, we learn to rest,
In the frost, we feel our best.

Echoes of Silence

In the stillness of the night,
Words drift softly, taking flight.
Whispers linger in the dark,
Lost in dreams, they leave their mark.

Echoes hum of things once said,
Stories linger, though all are dead.
Silence wraps the heart in peace,
From the noise, we seek release.

Memories dance on the cool air,
Carried gently, we lay bare.
In the quiet, truths will weave,
All that we dare to believe.

Shadows soften, fears grow small,
In silence, we can hear the call.
Life unfolds in a gentle way,
Through echoes that forever stay.

So let the whispers guide your soul,
In the silence, find your role.
For in every hushed refrain,
Lies the wisdom of the rain.

The Brew of Winter Nights

A kettle sings on the warm stove,
Steam swirls like stories we wove.
Cinnamon dances, sweet delight,
Filling hearts on a winter's night.

Fires crackle with tender glow,
Casting shadows that softly flow.
Mugs are lifted, warmth in hand,
A moment cherished, simply planned.

Frosty windows, a world of white,
As stars twinkle in the night.
Hot cocoa swirls, rich and deep,
In this comfort, secrets keep.

Outside, the snowflakes whirl and play,
Inside, our laughter lights the way.
Each sip a memory, deeply sown,
In the brew, we're never alone.

So let us gather, tooth and nail,
Under winter's soft, silver veil.
With every pour, our spirits rise,
In each moment, love never dies.

Dappled in Frost

Morning breaks with a silver hand,
Frost glistens, a fairyland.
Each blade of grass a work of art,
Nature's canvas, warms the heart.

Sunlight kisses, melts away,
The icy dreams of yesterday.
Petals shimmer, depths revealed,
A hidden beauty, gently healed.

Birds alight on branches bare,
Filling the quiet with sweet air.
Songs of hope in soft repose,
Amongst the joy that nature shows.

Frosted windows, warm inside,
In these moments, we abide.
Each breath taken, crisp and bright,
Dappled in frost, our spirits light.

So let us walk on this lace spun ground,
In whispers soft, love will abound.
For beauty's found in every hue,
When hearts embrace the world anew.

Frozen Murmurs

In the hush of a frozen stream,
Whispers echo like a dream.
Nature holds her breath so tight,
Underneath the soft moonlight.

Icicles hang like frozen tears,
Hiding laughter, holding fears.
From the depths, a murmur's song,
Calls us forth where we belong.

Beneath the frost, the world will sigh,
Echoing stories, passing by.
In every glimmer, secrets stay,
Frozen words have much to say.

So tread gently on this ground,
In the silence, beauty's found.
With each heartbeat, feel it grow,
A tapestry of frost and flow.

For in the still, our hearts may find,
A timeless bond, forever blind.
In frozen murmurs, spirits blend,
Whispering tales that never end.

Beneath a Frozen Sky

Beneath a sky of frost and gray,
The whispers of the wind at play,
I see the world in quiet white,
A stillness held, soft and bright.

The trees stand tall, their limbs adorned,
In icy coats, a beauty mourned,
Each breath a cloud, as time does freeze,
In frozen dreams, I find my peace.

The stars emerge in velvet night,
Their glimmers dance, a silver light,
A universe of silent sighs,
Where dreams and wishes freely rise.

While shadows loom, so deep and vast,
They cradle secrets of the past,
Yet in this chill, I feel the glow,
Of warmth within the coldest blow.

Beneath this sky, in silence grand,
I find my heart, I take a stand,
In every flake, a story told,
Beneath a sky both fierce and bold.

Hush of the Cold

In winter's grasp, the world is still,
A hush descends upon the hill,
Each flake a whisper, soft and light,
Wrapping the earth in purest white.

The trees like sentinels stand tall,
Their branches draped, a crystal shawl,
A quiet peace in morning's glow,
As gentle winds begin to blow.

The river flows in shimmering dreams,
Reflecting light in playful beams,
In frozen pools, the silence reigns,
While nature sleeps, her heart contains.

The distant mountains gently gleam,
Encapsulated in winter's dream,
With every breath, the cold invites,
A tranquil calm in starry nights.

Hush now, the world, in frosty lace,
In every glance, a sacred space,
For in this cold, I find my song,
The hush of winter, soft and strong.

Gleaming Shadows

In twilight's glow, the shadows gleam,
A dance of light, a fleeting dream,
With whispers caught in golden rays,
The world alive in dusky plays.

The night descends, a velvet sheet,
As stars awake, their song discreet,
Each twinkle tells a story grand,
In gleams and sparkles, hand in hand.

The moonlight spills on surfaces bright,
Transforming edge and shape with light,
A silver trail through darkened lanes,
Where silent echoes leave their stains.

The trees cast silhouettes so bold,
In shapes and forms, their mysteries hold,
Each rustle in the evening's grasp,
A secret shared, a moment clasped.

In gleaming shadows, life unfolds,
A tapestry of stories told,
Where light and dark in harmony blend,
Together woven, until the end.

Embrace of the North

In the north, where silence reigns,
The air is crisp, the heart contains,
With every breath, a chill invites,
The quiet beauty of cold nights.

Snowflakes dance on winter's breath,
In dazzling forms of joy and jest,
Each one a story, unique, apart,
An artful print on nature's heart.

The aurora paints the sky in hues,
Of vibrant greens and softest blues,
A cosmic ballet, a tranquil sight,
That shimmers softly through the night.

The mountains rise in noble grace,
In icy peaks, I find my place,
Where echoes linger, wild and free,
Embraced by nature's mystery.

In the north, I feel alive,
With every chill, my spirit thrives,
The embrace of the cold, a tender kiss,
In winter's hold, I find my bliss.

The Icy Touch

The winter breathes a chilling air,
Its icy fingers pull and tear.
Blankets of white cover the ground,
A frozen world, silence found.

Each tree wears crystals in the sun,
A glistening beauty just begun.
Footsteps crunch under the weight,
Echoes of a frosty fate.

The river sleeps beneath its ice,
Whispers of the cold entice.
Nature pauses, holds her breath,
In this moment, life meets death.

Stars twinkle in a velvet sky,
As frosty winds begin to sigh.
The night is deep, a fourth dimension,
In this realm, there's no intention.

Spring may come, but now it's cold,
In winter's grasp, stories unfold.
The icy touch, both cruel and fair,
A dance of beauty laid so bare.

Silence in Snow

In quiet drifts, the world is hushed,
A blanket of snow, the earth is flushed.
Whispers dance on frozen air,
Silence reigns, beyond compare.

Softly falling, flakes descend,
Each one tells a tale, my friend.
A moment stilled, with bated breath,
In this quiet, we find depth.

The moonlight glows, a silver seam,
Every shadow, every dream.
In the embrace of winter night,
The world transforms in purest light.

Footprints vanish, time is slow,
In the stillness, secrets grow.
Winter whispers through the trees,
A tranquil hush upon the breeze.

Let us linger, pause and feel,
The beauty that the snow can steal.
For in this calm, we find our way,
Silence in snow, a perfect stay.

Crystal Veil

A crystal veil drapes o'er the land,
Sparkling diamonds in winter's hand.
Nature's art, displayed with grace,
Each glittering flake, a fleeting trace.

Trees adorned in frosted white,
Glisten softly in the night.
Whispers of ice in the biting air,
A world transformed, beyond compare.

The morning sun, a golden eye,
Melts the dreams of winter's high.
Reflections dance upon the stream,
In this moment, all is dream.

Birds in flight leave trails of song,
In crystal worlds, where they belong.
Echoes linger in the cold,
Stories waiting to be told.

So pause awhile and take it in,
The crystal veil, where dreams begin.
The beauty that this season brings,
In winter's hand, the heart takes wings.

Winter's Lullaby

Snowflakes fall, a gentle sigh,
Nature sings a soft lullaby.
A blanket muffles every sound,
In this hush, peace is found.

The stars twinkle like distant dreams,
In winter's grasp, a space that gleams.
Fires crackle, warmth inside,
Against the cold, we shall abide.

Moonlit paths lead hearts astray,
In the night, thoughts drift away.
Cold winds whisper through the trees,
Caressing branches, swaying ease.

Underneath the blanket white,
The earth is cradled, safe at night.
In this dreamscape, time stands still,
Winter's lullaby does fulfill.

So close your eyes, let visions play,
In this silence, we find our way.
Winter hums her gentle tune,
A lullaby beneath the moon.

Woven in Winter Light

The sun dips low in frosty gleam,
Snowflakes dance, a sparkling dream.
Whispers of wind through trees so bare,
Nature's quilt in the crisp air.

Footprints trace where lovers tread,
In the silence, soft words are said.
Shadows blend with the twilight glow,
Hearts entwined in the evening's snow.

Each breath a mist in the twilight hue,
Wrapped in warmth, a world anew.
Stars peek forth from a velvet night,
Together we bask in winter's light.

Branches hold the weight of white,
Glowing softly under gentle light.
A canvas stretched from here to there,
Woven whispers fill the chilled air.

As dawn creeps in, the world awakes,
Underneath, a stillness breaks.
Embraced by all, this winter scene,
In nature's arms, so pure, serene.

Chilling Reflections

Ponds mirror skies of slate and grey,
Frigid waters where shadows play.
A stillness wraps the frozen ground,
In every breath, a crisp sound found.

Icicles hang like chandeliers,
Nature's art through the quiet years.
Leaves long gone, yet memories stay,
Reflecting on this hushed ballet.

Meandering paths through the forest crisp,
Fingers numb from the icy grip.
Within the stillness, echoes call,
As winter weaves a spell on all.

Lights that flicker in the dark,
Candle flames that brave the stark.
Laughter mingles with the cold,
Chilling reflections yet untold.

In the air, a promise lies,
Beneath the frost, the life that sighs.
For every bite of winter's chill,
Awakens spring with warming thrill.

Enchantment in White

A flurry falls with joyous cheer,
Cloaking the world in blankets sheer.
Each flake unique, a story spun,
In winter's magic, all has begun.

The trees adorned in pearly frost,
Beauty found in what was lost.
Paths are lined with glimmering glow,
Whispers sweet in the falling snow.

Children laugh and softly glide,
On sleds that carry them, side by side.
Snowmen rise with a carol's glee,
Enchantment reigns in this jubilee.

Stars above in the night so bright,
Guiding dreams with their gentle light.
A universe painted, pure and white,
Awakening hearts on this magical night.

As shadows stretch and greet the dawn,
The world awakens, winter drawn.
In every flake, in every sight,
Lies a promise of enchantment, bright.

A Blanket of Glimmering Ice

Crystals shimmer on branches bare,
Nature's art in the still, cold air.
Beneath the sheen lies a world asleep,
A silent promise for time to keep.

Underneath, the earth holds tight,
Dreaming softly through the night.
A blanket wraps the sleeping land,
Softly stitched by a gentle hand.

Footsteps crunch on paths so bright,
Where shadows dance in the fading light.
Each reflection, a story told,
Glimmers of magic, a sight to behold.

As stars twinkle in the endless sky,
Hope rises like a whispered sigh.
This frozen world, a crystal sphere,
With glimmering ice that draws us near.

And as the winter's breath does pause,
Nature's beauty brings its cause.
Wrapped in stillness, we see what's nice,
Our hearts unite in this glimmering ice.

Echoes of Ice

In stillness we tread, whispers so cold,
Echoes of glaciers, stories retold.
Frozen in time, moments held tight,
Beneath a pale moon, bathed in soft light.

A shiver runs deep, beneath the white crust,
Nature's own canvas, painted in trust.
Crystals of frost, like stars in the night,
Glisten and sparkle, a beautiful sight.

The winds carry secrets, tales of the past,
In the heart of the ice, shadows are cast.
Each creak of the snow, each sigh of the chill,
Calls forth a memory, the whispering thrill.

Time dances slowly, in winter's embrace,
A world wrapped in silence, a tranquil space.
We breathe in the echoes, the stories that bind,
Lost in the stillness, our souls intertwined.

Through valleys of frost, we wander and roam,
In the heart of this stillness, we finally feel home.
With each breath of frost, our worries held tight,
Echoes of ice guide us, through the long night.

Shivering Stillness

Amidst the white drifts, the world holds its breath,
In shivering stillness, a dance with death.
Snowflakes like whispers, descend from the sky,
Painting the earth with a soft lullaby.

Branches adorned with a delicate lace,
A shroud of pure silence, time slows its pace.
Footsteps are muffled, as hearts start to race,
In the beauty of winter, we find our place.

Frost-kissed horizons, the sun peeks through,
A canvas of wonders, painted in blue.
Each flake a reminder, of moments so rare,
In the shivering stillness, we linger, aware.

Cold winds may howl, but here we are warm,
Cradled by nature, safe from the storm.
Lost in the frosty embrace we create,
In the depth of the silence, we patiently wait.

As twilight descends, a hush fills the air,
Stars flicker awake, with glimmers so rare.
In shivering stillness, we find our delight,
Wrapped in the coziness of a winter night.

Glacial Reverie

In dreams of the ice, we drift far away,
Where glaciers whisper and shadows play.
Crystalline visions, a world bathed in blue,
In glacial reverie, we find what is true.

Mountains of silence, reach high to the sky,
A sanctuary formed, where eagles can fly.
Each breath of the cold, fills our souls with peace,
In a realm of stillness, all worries cease.

Frozen reflections, in pools calm and deep,
Guarding the secrets that nature will keep.
Time drips like water, in rhythmic embrace,
In the heart of the glacier, we find our grace.

With each passing moment, the world feels so vast,
In this glacial dreamscape, we're free from the past.
Awash in the beauty, we surrender and sway,
To the whispers of ice that guide our way.

As night deepens softly, the stars shine so bright,
In glacial reverie, we cherish the night.
Together we journey, in silence we roam,
In the heart of the cold, we create our home.

The Pale Blanket

A pale blanket covers the land soft and white,
Whispers of winter embrace the night.
Each flake a soft kiss, a gentle sigh,
In the hush of the moment, time passes by.

Under the vast canopy of diamond-spun skies,
The world feels enchanted, where magic lies.
Footprints in snow, a pathway to chase,
Wrapped in the blanket, we find our place.

Trees draped in silver, a shimmering glow,
Silent observances, as breezes flow.
The stillness around us, a symphony plays,
In the echoing silence, our spirits to raise.

The moon's gentle light spills over the land,
A serene invitation, a warm, guiding hand.
Each moment a treasure, in the heart of the night,
Under the pale blanket, the world feels just right.

So here we will linger, 'neath stars shining bright,
In this winter wonder, our hearts take flight.
Together we dance in the soft silver glow,
In the warmth of the pale blanket, love starts to grow.

A Chilling Embrace

In the still of night, whispers creep,
Winter's breath in shadows deep.
Silence wrapped in icy song,
A chilling embrace, the night is long.

Stars twinkle like diamonds bright,
Beneath the cloak of the frosty night.
Branches bow with a silver frost,
In this quiet, warmth is lost.

The world is hushed, no sound to break,
Just the crunch of steps on a frozen lake.
Moonlight dances on a frozen sea,
In this stillness, the heart feels free.

Every breath is a sigh so cold,
In the chill, stories are told.
Nature rests in its frozen bed,
While dreams of warmth linger overhead.

So take a moment, breathe in deep,
In winter's hold, our secrets keep.
A chilling embrace wraps us tight,
For dawn will bring a softer light.

Veils of Snow

Veils of snow, a whispering glow,
Cover the world, silent and slow.
Blankets of white on fields so wide,
Nature cloaked in a wintry pride.

Footprints fade in the softest hush,
As trees stand tall in a gentle crush.
Soft as feathers, the flakes descend,
In this stillness, time seems to blend.

Evening falls with a twinkling charm,
Moonlight weaves a magic warm.
In the shadows, secrets blend,
Veils of snow, where dreams extend.

The air is crisp, a sweet delight,
Under the stars so brilliantly bright.
In each flurry, a story spun,
Veils of snow, where all begun.

As dawn breaks, the colors rise,
With golden rays to pierce the skies.
But in the night, we'll always know,
The beauty held in veils of snow.

Lull Before Thaw

In the hush before the thaw,
Nature breathes without a flaw.
A quiet pause, the world holds still,
Waiting for warmth, a whispered thrill.

Branches bare, yet buds are near,
With every breath, spring draws near.
The frost will fade, the warmth will rise,
In this moment, the heart complies.

Clouds drift soft in a pastel hue,
While shadows stretch, embracing new.
A lull exists, so sweet and rare,
An eager calm fills the air.

The earth sleeps with a tender grace,
In dreams of the sun's warm embrace.
Patience grows with every sigh,
In this lull, let spirits fly.

Soon the colors will break the gray,
Life will bloom, as night turns day.
But in this moment, we stand and breathe,
A lull before we weave.

Frost on Winter's Heart

A crackling sound, the frost takes hold,
Winter's heart beats brave and bold.
Land adorned in glistening white,
A tapestry woven in the fading light.

Each breath forms a cloud, hanging faint,
Nature whispers, serene and quaint.
In the chill, there's a beauty rare,
Frost on winter's heart, beyond compare.

Shadows stretch as daylight dims,
With every moment, the cold exhales hymns.
Ice coats the world in delicate layers,
A reminder of nature's silent prayers.

In the quiet, find a spark,
Of warmth that glows within the dark.
Frost may bite, yet also reveal,
The magic in winter, a gentle seal.

So let us wander through this chill,
With hearts aglow, and spirits still.
In every flake, a story starts,
In frost, we find winter's heart.

Secrets of the Snowfall

Whispers dance on frosty air,
Silent stories everywhere.
Snowflakes twirl, a soft ballet,
In their grace, the world will sway.

Each flake holds a tale untold,
Of winter nights and dreams of gold.
They blanket earth in hushed delight,
Tucking secrets in the night.

Underneath the silver sheen,
Nature's wonder, pure and keen.
Branches bow with heavy loads,
Guardians of the hidden roads.

As dawn breaks, a spark of light,
Reveals the magic, pure and bright.
The silent echoes start to fade,
Yet in our hearts, their paths are laid.

Thus, we gather 'round the fire,
With longing thoughts that never tire.
For every snowfall brings a chance,
To lose ourselves in nature's dance.

Crystalized Memories

Frozen gems on windowpanes,
Each with stories, joys, and pains.
Past embraces in their light,
Fleeting moments, pure and bright.

With every sparkle, whispers rise,
Echoes trapped in winter's sighs.
Memories swirl like drifting snow,
In their depths, our heartbeats flow.

The chill brings warmth, in its own way,
A tender heart that learns to sway.
Crystal visions, clear and bold,
We relive tales we've yet to hold.

In quiet hours, reflections gleam,
Shaping shadows of the dream.
With every flake that falls at night,
Time stands still, the world feels right.

Thus, we cherish all we've known,
Each crystal thought, a seed we've sown.
In winter's arms, we find our place,
In crystalized memories, we embrace.

The Winter Veil

Softly draped in white so fine,
Nature's hush, a sacred sign.
Blankets cover earth and sky,
Underneath, dreams quietly lie.

The world wrapped in a tranquil glow,
Hidden whispers, secrets flow.
Trees stand tall, adorned in lace,
Nature's touch, a soft embrace.

Every breath, a frosty mist,
Moments linger, too sweet to miss.
Below the layers, life persists,
In quiet realms, the heart insists.

As shadows lengthen, twilight calls,
Under the veil, the magic sprawls.
Stars peep through the winter's shroud,
Linking hearts in starlit crowd.

Thus, we wander, hand in hand,
Through frost-kissed woods, a timeless land.
In winter's veil, we'll find our way,
In peace and love, we choose to stay.

Veins of Ice

Through the trees, a chill reborn,
Nature's pulse, a silent thorn.
Beneath the frost, life waits in pause,
Heartbeats slowing, by nature's laws.

Crystals gleam in the morning light,
Veins of ice, both fierce and bright.
Every pathway, etched and clear,
Tells a story we hold dear.

Frozen rivers, silent as night,
Reflecting dreams in silver light.
Each icy thread runs deep and wise,
Binding souls beneath the skies.

In the stillness, we find our breath,
Amidst the beauty, we embrace death.
Life's rhythm dances, ebb and flow,
In veins of ice, our spirits glow.

Thus, we wander, with hearts so bold,
In winter's grip, our stories told.
Through every moment, crystallized grace,
In veins of ice, we find our place.

Shadows of a Snowy Heart

Beneath the chill of winter's sigh,
Whispers of dreams begin to fly.
Footsteps trace in drifts of white,
Lost in the shimmers of soft moonlight.

In the stillness, secrets hide,
Frozen tears where hopes abide.
A heartbeat echoes, silent shout,
Amidst the snowflakes swirling about.

Embers glow in the frosty air,
Memories linger, fragile and rare.
Shadows dance in the quiet night,
Yearning for warmth, for love's delight.

Each snowflake tells a story old,
In patterns soft, in glimmers bold.
A heart that shivers, yet still feels,
Underneath the frozen wheels.

In twilight's embrace, dreams gently part,
Leaving traces on a snowy heart.
The world drifts away in silent grace,
As shadows whisper in their place.

Glistening Silence

In the hour where time stands still,
A glistening hush, a winter thrill.
The world adorned in crystals bright,
A canvas stretched in silver light.

Each breath released, a foggy sigh,
A shimmer falls, a gentle cry.
Whispers of frost on the frozen ground,
In the stillness, peace is found.

Snowflakes spin in a twirling dance,
Nature's beauty, a fleeting chance.
Glistening moments, soft and shy,
Captured dreams that softly fly.

Stars twinkle above in the night's embrace,
Lighting paths in this tranquil space.
A symphony crafted by the night,
In glistening silence, pure delight.

With every drift, with every sigh,
The world glimmers, as shadows die.
In this realm of soft, white dreams,
Peace whispers in the silenced streams.

The Silent Caress

In twilight's glow, a soft caress,
A gentle touch in the cold's embrace.
Snowflakes fall like whispered vows,
Blanketing earth with silent rows.

Frost-kissed air holds secrets deep,
Where quiet spirits play and leap.
The world slows down, breaths intertwine,
In moments lost, our hearts align.

Beneath the stars, we find our place,
In the stillness, a warm embrace.
Nature's hush cradles our fears,
As winter's magic draws us near.

Every heartbeat, a tender song,
Echoes of where we both belong.
The silent caress of the night,
Gifts us hope, ignites the light.

So let the snowflakes gently fall,
And wrap us in their softest thrall.
For in this stillness, hearts confess,
The beauty found in quiet rest.

Echoes in the Frost

In the frost, where echoes play,
Chilled whispers dance at end of day.
The world shimmers in silver sheen,
Fragments of dreams, softly seen.

Amidst the trees, the shadows loom,
Carrying tales of winter's gloom.
Footsteps fade on paths frost-kissed,
Lost in the magic of the mist.

Each breath holds a story, yet untold,
Of longing hearts and empires bold.
The echo of laughter in the night,
Fading slowly, out of sight.

Underneath stars that brightly gleam,
Woven tales of a distant dream.
The frost holds secrets, pure and deep,
In its embrace, the world will sleep.

So listen close to the frosty air,
For echoes linger, always there.
In the quiet, the whispers ride,
As winter's heart and dreams collide.

The Magic of Icy Nights

Stars glitter above, so bright and clear,
The world wrapped in frost, a magical sphere.
Whispers in the wind, tales of the freeze,
Moments suspended, nature's sweet tease.

Moonlight dances on the frozen streams,
Each sparkling crystal captures our dreams.
Footsteps crunch softly on the snow's embrace,
In this icy wonder, we find our place.

The breath of the night, so crisp and still,
Fills our hearts with wonder, a gentle thrill.
Each flake that descends, a unique delight,
The beauty of winter, the magic of night.

Candles flicker, casting warm, soft glows,
Underneath the stars, where the cool wind blows.
Cozy and calm, we gather around,
In the magic of icy nights, peace is found.

With every heartbeat, the silence sings,
Of moments shared, and the joy it brings.
In this tranquil realm, we find our way,
Wrapped in the magic of a winter's day.

The Beauty of Chill

A blanket of white covers the earth,
In the quiet of morning, there's whisper and mirth.
Frost clings to branches, a delicate lace,
In the beauty of chill, we find our grace.

Breath hangs like clouds in the frosty air,
Nature's stillness, a soft, gentle stare.
Each tree is a sculpture, each pathway a dream,
The beauty of chill flows like a stream.

Icicles dangle, like jewels on display,
Glistening under the sun's golden ray.
The world seems to pause in this winter's embrace,
In the beauty of chill, we find our place.

Warm hugs and laughter surround the cold,
Hot cocoa in hand, stories are told.
With each frosty breath, we cherish the thrill,
In the heart of winter, we savor the chill.

Snowflakes like feathers dance from the skies,
A wonderland formed, where the magic lies.
In every crisp moment, our spirits instill,
A love for the season, the beauty of chill.

Winter's Caress

Gentle winds whisper through the sleeping trees,
Winter's caress brings us to our knees.
Blankets of snow wrap the world so tight,
In this frozen wonderland, pure and white.

The silence is sacred, the air full of dreams,
Softly, the moonlight on glistening beams.
Each step in the snow leaves a mark of our grace,
In the soft embrace of winter's embrace.

Footprints lead onward to places unknown,
Where magic persists, and the heart finds its own.
Branches adorned with a crystalline glaze,
A picture of peace in a wintery haze.

Firelight flickers, casting shadows that play,
In the warmth of the hearth, we linger and stay.
With loved ones beside us, we gather and share,
The joy of the season, winter's sweet care.

Moments like these are treasures we keep,
In the heart of winter, where memories seep.
Through soft falling snow, hope begins to press,
In the powerful touch of winter's caress.

Whispered Chills

Whispers of winter breathe through the trees,
Carried on breezes, the softest of pleas.
Under a blanket of shimmering white,
The world slows down, resting in night.

Cold kisses dance on the skin, so sweet,
With each gentle touch, our hearts skip a beat.
In the hush of the evening, we pause to reflect,
On the magic of moments that winter can collect.

Candles aglow in the frosty air,
Flicker with stories we long to share.
In cozy corners, warmth wraps us tight,
Within the embrace of the oncoming night.

Snowflakes that flutter seem timeless and grand,
Delicate wonders fall, handcrafted by hand.
Within each small flake lies a promise, a thrill,
In the beauty and peace of whispered chills.

Holding on to dreams as the cold winds sigh,
With hearts intertwined, we watch the night fly.
And in every still moment, our spirits fulfill,
The joy and the magic of whispered chills.

Beneath the Frozen Veil

Whispers dance in silent air,
A land where dreams are rare.
Each flake a story, softly spun,
Beneath the veil, the world is one.

Trees wear coats of glimmering white,
Underneath a starry night.
Footprints echo on the ground,
In this peace, no word is found.

Frozen rivers, still as glass,
Time drifts slowly, moments pass.
A tranquil hush, a calming scene,
In this realm, we find serene.

Shadows stretch as daylight fades,
In icy whispers, secrets wade.
Life suspended in the freeze,
Beneath the veil, the heart's at ease.

So here we breathe, we pause, we dream,
In this world, a gentle gleam.
Together, lost in winter's grace,
Beneath the frozen veil, we trace.

Crystalline Dreams

In the hush of early morn,
Snowflakes whisper, soft and worn.
Each shimmer tells a tale anew,
Crystalline dreams in sparkling blue.

The world transformed, a canvas bright,
Underneath the pale moonlight.
Glistening paths invite the roam,
In silence, every heart finds home.

Frosted petals gently sigh,
Underneath the vast, wide sky.
With every breath, the magic grows,
In frozen beauty, nature glows.

Crystal lanterns softly blink,
Inviting us to pause and think.
In this dream, where moments sway,
We dance with joy, come what may.

So let us wander, hand in hand,
In crystalline dreams, forever stand.
Lost in wonder, time will freeze,
In this world, the soul finds ease.

Shiver of Dawn

The sun peeks through, a gentle rise,
In frosty breath, the morning sighs.
Shadows linger, softly fade,
As dawn awakens, light invade.

The world is wrapped in twilight glow,
Each moment whispers, soft and slow.
A shiver dances on the skin,
In golden light, the day begins.

Branches glisten, kissed by frost,
In this beauty, we're never lost.
With every ray, the chill retreats,
The warmth of life, a heart that beats.

Footsteps crunch on carpeted ground,
A symphony of silence found.
In the shiver of dawn's embrace,
New hopes arise, a freshened space.

Together we'll greet the day ahead,
With joy ignited, fears now shed.
In the shiver, our spirits soar,
With every dawn, we bloom once more.

Touched by Winter's Breath

Whispers linger in the air,
Every moment, light and rare.
Touched by winter's breath so sweet,
A magic found beneath our feet.

Snowflakes twirl, a ballet grand,
Painting beauty on the land.
In this wonder, hearts entwine,
Touched by gifts from the divine.

The chill wraps tight, a soft embrace,
A tranquil pause, a sacred space.
Each gust sings a lullaby,
In winter's arms, we learn to fly.

Frosty echoes of laughter spill,
In every heart, a cozy thrill.
Winter's breath, a tender touch,
In this solace, we find so much.

So let us dance where snowflakes gleam,
In a world spun from a dream.
Touched by winter, we'll never part,
In this beauty, we find our heart.